Biting
The
Sun

Twenty-five Years of

The Boston Haiku Society

edited by John Ziemba

Biting The Sun

ISBN:0692343903
ISBN-13:9780692343906

DEDICATION

The members of the Boston Haiku Society would like to express
their appreciation to the members of the Kaji Aso Studio, and
especially its administrator, Kate Finnegan, who has allowed us to
meet in what is basically her office for the past twenty-five years,
and has always provided us with support and encouragement.

CONTENTS

ACKNOWLEDGMENTS

We'd like to thank, once again, the members of the Kaji Aso Studio: to Kaji Aso and Kate Finnegan, who supported and fostered the BHS throughout its entire history; to Gary Tucker, a master painter who has provided cover art for the newsletters and was key in transferring Mr. Aso's sumie painting which appears on the cover to a format that could be reproduced as you see it. Also, to Raffael de Gruttola, who produced the BHS newsletter for years, and was able to provide a cohesive history of our group from its beginnings until now; and to Charles Trumbull, who, in his efforts to archive English language haiku, created lists of individual poets' haiku from our BHS newsletters, which were invaluable in creating collections of our members who are no longer with us; and to the BHS members who volunteered their time to edit, proofread, and buffalo fellow members into keeping deadlines: Brad Bennett, Kay Higuchi, Larry Rungren, Zeke Vayman, and John Ziemba, the latter who edited and compiled this book, as well as went over deadline by, oh, just about a year.

An Evening in Autumn:
How We Started, What We Are

秋深き隣は何をする人ぞ

aki fukaki tonari wa nani o suru hito zo

autumn deepens
my neighbor,
what is he doing?
—Matsuo Basho

Fall, 1988. In the previous year, I wrote a letter to Bill Higginson, whose *Haiku Handbook* I had recently read, asking what I could do to make a career of haiku. He seemed like the go-to guy in American haiku at the time, and was no doubt enjoying a fabulous life spreading the gospel of 'the wordless poem.' Bill, surely in a spirit of great magnanimity, actually wrote back, advising me that one doesn't make a career of haiku. It's a wonderful thing kid, but don't give up your day job. Keep writing, but make sure you know which side your bread is buttered on, or so I took it, so I recall.

I was incensed. I took Higginson to be a Philistine, and felt patronized. Did he really think I believed I could earn a tidy living in the haiku racket? Haiku is the poetry of poverty and simplicity. I hadn't gone to twelve years of Catholic schooling for nothing! I was prepared to make the sacrifice, and he thought, he…he…!

Of course, should any youngster ask me the same question in these latter years of my life, I would stress the same thing. Higginson had a good point, and was good and wise to apprise me of the harsh realities of the haiku biz. Nobody reads poetry, and only a small percent of those read haiku! But I was on fire with haiku. I'd been a member of the Kaji Aso Studio for the past six years, leading the poetry workshop for three or four, and had just gotten back from my second trip to Japan. Half of the month I'd spent there was dedicated to tracking down Bashō, in Kyoto, in his hometown of Iga Ueno, in Otsu, where he wrote the *Genjuan,* or "Hermitage of Illusion," and then up to Sendai—*Oku no Hosomichi* country, where I visited Matsushima, then up to Kessenuma, where I was hosted by Robert Reed, a former Kaji Aso Studio member who had married and settled in Japan. He took me to Hiraizumi, then to the Edo guard house where Bashō had written "fleas, lice/ horse pissing/by my pillow." We parted ways at the Mogami River, from which I took a bus to Haguro and Gassan in Yamagata, then swung back east to pass by Yamadera ("the stillness/piercing the stones/the cries of cicada").

On my way back to the U.S., haiku caused me some awkwardness. I had been making my living as a housepainter at the time, and had considerable difficulty convincing a proto-Homeland Security officer at O'Hare that I, a humble tradesman, had spent a month in Japan in the name of haiku! Fess up, kid, why were you *really* there? I tried to tell him about the Kaji Aso Studio, where we had just begun the Kaji Aso Studio Haiku Contest. (My inquisitor finally gave up in frustration, convinced that while I was probably up to no good, it was simple folly and I would harm no one but myself.)

Back in the States, with the subscription to *Frogpond* that I'd invested in, I received a mailing list of haiku poets around the country. To these folks we mailed out, one by one, invitations to take part in our competition; I would not have had the audacity to begin such a venture without the guidance of Kaji Aso, of the aforementioned Kaji Aso Studio. At the time of this writing, it's been eight years since Mr. Aso passed away, but it really seems like no time at all since he was in his prime...and what a prime it was! He was an internationally famous painter, had begun his own school in a foreign country. This school, happened to be around the corner from my apartment on Gainsborough Street, where I used to dash off thirty or forty sumi paintings at a sitting with my China-town-bought inkstone, a ream of typing paper—rice paper too expensive—and a couple of precious books on the topic. One of these books actually listed places where you could study Japanese ink-brush painting; there was a grand total of about a dozen locales in all. Over half were in California, a couple in New York City, and one serendipitously situated a two minute walk around the corner from me. The place with the weird name that I'd always assumed was a cult or martial-arts studio was in reality a bustling little artists' cooperative. At the time, Kaji Aso was teaching at the School of the Museum of Fine Arts, but insisted that art was not something confined to a garret—or, I suppose, a hermitage in the autumn landscape. He led his students in runnings of the Boston Marathon (and continued to do so until a year before his passing), conducted canoe/kayak trips down the Mississippi, Connecticut, Shinano (Japan), and Seine rivers (up until that point, after which he added the Volga, the Nile, the Suwannee, and Tagus), was an accomplished operatic tenor—many is the night I saw him finish teaching at the Studio, paint for hours, then head down to the gallery's piano and practice scales and arias until the wee hours. He also had a seemingly encyclopedic knowledge of Japanese culture, including Japanese literature—with him anchoring the contest, an upstart such as myself could muster the chutzpah to send invitations out to some of the heavy hitters of the haiku world at the time.

And it was in this spirit that, after I'd returned from Japan in the early autumn of 1988, I began to wonder what my fellow New England haiku poets were doing. There was a Haiku Society of America. There was a Haiku Canada (I believe it was in May that I sojourned up to Aylmer, Canada with the legendary Arizona Zipper to attend a meeting and met some wonderful folks up there) and thought that, surely, the Boston area must have some talent, or at least plenty of folks interested in haiku. And so I scoured the mailing list and found, to my recollection, around twenty names, including a mellifluous one that I'd heard before: Raffael de Gruttola. He'd published quite a bit and was a big name in the HSA. It was on an evening in early November, I'm fairly certain, that we met in the same room in which we meet now. It was not a third Saturday, not at 2:00, but about the same number of poets that meet now met then. Those I am certain about: Larry Rungren, a tall, blonde, soft spoken mid-westerner who I could tell really got haiku; Brett Peruzzi, an bearded, witty gent with an urban bent to his haiku; Glenn Gustaffson, a quiet Boston native with a quirky, poignant style...and then memory fails. Was June Moreau there, one of the most original, imaginative haiku poets I've ever met? Did Balasz Kozaras make it that first night—a brilliant Hungarian high school student recently come to the U.S.? Donald Kelly—I think he must have been there. Donald, who was called away so soon... At any rate, Kaji Aso was there, and if he were not, I very much doubt that my presence would have kept most of the afore-mentioned folks coming for years; Mr. Aso would attract many more over the years. His support, wisdom, and confidence proved to be both lodestone and cornerstone for our little group. I was nervous; I wore a tie; and I cannot remember a single thing of significance I said that night (most likely because I didn't say anything of significance). But we did manage to make an agreement to meet regularly. Perhaps it was even then that the time that we've set aside for our meetings—third Saturday of the month at 2:00— came into being. We began our tradition of going around the room and presenting our haiku for discussion. I can't recall whose idea it was to pull over one of the many easels at the Studio, write haiku with a magic marker and post it so all could see the poem in question. Soon, we were printing up the haiku presented at our meetings in a newsletter, misinterpreted by some misguided souls as a publication (yes, there are some who would not allow us to distribute these haiku to members only as minutes of our meeting, and refuse them for publication—they know who they are!). Perhaps this was because Raffael, who came to be the one who generously devoted his time to putting the newsletter together and sending it out, graced one of the tri-fold sides with an illustration, often original, giving it a publication-type look. At any rate, the newsletter has since become a digital record and serves as a wonderful record of all our gatherings. Raffael has the complete set someplace, which, if there's any justice, will one day grace the archives of some international haiku museum.

How to characterize our meetings? I like to think of it as a haiku forum, a place for people with various views of haiku, various backgrounds in writing, to get together, share their work, and find out what does and doesn't work. Sometimes a haiku is read and met with nothing more than a few grunts of approval. Maybe an expression or two of appreciation. That's usually a good sign—there's nothing more to add to it, nothing that can be omitted, and the writer can be said to have communicated his or her experience beautifully. Other times, lines get shuffled around—first to last, last to first—articles are fought over; dashes, ellipses, tildes, etc, get darted about the room. The author sometimes gratefully adopts the suggestions, other times battles to explain why the poem makes no sense in any way other than the way he or she has rendered it. Political arguments have emerged, views on the nature of art get bandied about, and I suppose that we occasionally get side-tracked from the business at hand: haiku. To me, however, this kind of exchange is the summit of poetic expression and communication. One can see before one's own eyes how a poem plays out in the minds of others. Even the most careful craftsman has blind spots and can never completely determine how much of the intended image or nuance is truly there on the page. That is why it is essential to show our work to others—and after all, isn't that what haiku has always been at its core? A way to share a moment of lived experience using language—in the most pared-down, bare-bones but evocative language possible? You can submit your haiku to a journal and have it pass before the eyes of hundreds (I was tempted to write thousands, but alas…), but that pales next to the experience of exposing your work to a group of poets who care as much about the medium as you do, and are eager to help you make the most of your core idea. I suppose this is how things were done in Bashō's day, but we, fortunately or unfortunately, have no such leaders or masters. Discipleship is a uniquely Japanese feature, manifesting itself in all of Japan's traditional arts. As products of western culture, particularly, that of a liberal democracy, we stand as equals. So, if a novice reader, in spite of the protests of a cadre of old veterans, insists that his or her haiku goes in the newsletter as is, in it goes.

Within a year or two after our first meeting, we were giving readings: I recall one in May at Arnold Arboretum, a combination of flower-viewing and haiku, another a year or so later at the Middle East Café in Central Square, Cambridge, at which the few catty hecklers who emerged (haiku was simply too goody-goody and apolitical for them) were quelled by the lovely, mysterious readings in Japanese of Junko Ibara. She would half-read, half sing the classical Japanese haiku in Japanese, then after a healthy pause, the translation would be given. A positive "ahhhhhh" could often be heard. I like to think that a few of the scoffers might be reading and writing haiku today. Also, we began collecting our work and printing the occasional chapbook: *The Ant's Afternoon, Handfuls of Stars, Voice of the Peeper,* and *Windflow.*

And so we continued through the nineties, meeting regularly, sometimes tightly packed into the modestly-sized meeting room, at other times with only a few members in attendance. During this time, Zinovy "Zeke" Vayman began to attend our meetings, soon becoming a poet well known throughout the world, founding haiku societies in Russia and Israel and attending conferences in Europe and Japan. Judson Evans, the director of Liberal Arts at Boston Conservatory, also joined us, enriching our palette with his extensive background in poetry in general and his ground-breaking experiments in haibun and video haiku. Later, Zinovy Vayman returned from visiting me during my stay in Japan with a new bride, Kay Higuchi, whose knowledge of the Japanese language and *gendai*, or modern, haiku has enriched our meetings immeasurably.

In 1995, I left Boston to attend graduate school in Pittsburgh, and after that was off to Japan for what turned out to be a nine year stint of teaching English. I finally returned in 2007 to find the Boston Haiku Society thriving, although not unchanged. I wish to make it clear that, although I had set the ball in motion, I was never the leader; Raffael de Gruttola, extremely prolific and well-connected, kept everything humming quite nicely (see his version of the history) in my absence, and the BHS flourished. While I was gone, haiku stars like Karen Klein, Jeanne Martin, Richard St Clair and Ken Carrier had joined us, and since I've been back, we've welcomed relative newcomers to haiku like Gwenn Gurnack, Shawna Carboni, Mike Cerone, and Brad Bennett, and watched as they have become skilled practitioners of the form. We added another key Japanese member, Reiko Seymour, and her Japanese speaking husband Tom Seymour, who keep our roots in the Japanese form strong. We miss the presence of Kaji Aso, but show no signs of slowing down (although our average age seems to have climbed a bit!). But I have no doubt that the next decade, and the decade after that, will find a Boston Haiku Society, a group of passionate lovers and crafters of this idiosyncratic Japanese form that somehow, people all over the world recognize as poetry in its quintessence, worth study, worth writing, and worth gathering together to share.

John Ziemba

History of the Boston Haiku Society

The by-laws of the Boston Haiku Society were written in November of 1988 with the original members of the group of haiku poets. This group of poets included Kaji Aso, the visionary founder, teacher, and artist of the Kaji Aso Studio, John Ziemba, Raffael de Gruttola, Lawrence Rungren, Donald Kelly, June Moreau, and Balazs Kozaras all who were part of the original members.

Shortly thereafter in 1989 other members joined and included Kathy Reynolds, David Schuster, Glen Gustafson, John King, Brett Peruzzi, Zeke Vayman, and Paul David Mena. These poets met on a monthly basis usually on the third Saturday of each month at the Kaji Aso Studio at St. Stephen's Street in Boston's *Back Bay*, as the area is still called today.

Through all these years the poets have met on the third Saturday of each month to present and discuss their haiku. Although we have never labeled ourselves as a "school," we are aware of the different stylistic trends of haiku, tanka, senryu, haibun, and renku throughout the haiku world. Our fascination remains in the immediacy of those special moments of which we write, and our individual perceptions of them.

Our meetings are lively and our critiques of each other's haiku are positive and perceptive. Members consider the significant meaning in the haiku and the revisions that many original haiku undergo as they are transformed into sharper and more poignant observations during the groups review. Often small changes are made that insure the true nature of the observation and the originality of the perceived moment of the poet.

17

In some cases a consensus of opinion is considered; however, the author has the final say as to the meaning of his or her original observation and whether the revision is accepted or denied by the poet. On-line email copies of the month's haiku are then sent to all members who have an email account.

Over the years, distinctive styles of writing have occurred and individual poets notice the originality of each member's unique take on life through both objective and subjective interpretations of nature. Each poet has his or her own and different approach or style to meaning and this phenomena is exciting to other members who learn different ways that individual observations of nature take on the character of the writers.

Through the years, the Boston Haiku Society has set a standard for excellent haiku as well as for the other Japanese forms of poetry that have become popular in the United States including renku, haibun, haiga, and senryu.

In 2001 the Studio and the BHS was host to the Haiku North America Conference that attracted poets throughout the United States, Canada, Europe, and Japan. Over 150 poets attended. The Conference participants introduced many new approaches to not only haiku, but demonstrated many aspects of Japanese culture including bonsai and lectures by prominent scholars about the different styles of the major Japanese art forms.

The Studio also coordinates haiku workshops at the Studio on Tuesday Evenings coordinated by John Ziemba. This activity has become popular not only for haiku poets but poets interested in this unique form of poetry that predates the world's interest in haiku.

Raffael de Gruttola

HAIKU: A Conversation

"Biting The Sun? How'd you come up with *that* title?"

"It comes from one of Kaji Aso's poems: "open mouthed/biting the morning sun/winter carp." Read the introduction for more info on him. First of all, we wanted to give Mr Aso some credit because he was certainly a big influence in the creation and growth of the Boston Haiku Society. Second, 'biting the sun' is kind of a metaphor—if you can accept that in a book of haiku—of how haiku poets try to nibble off bits of the ineffable, capture the uncapturable. Also, Japan is the land of the rising sun, as well as the origin of haiku, and we here in Boston, so spatially, culturally, and linguistically distant, are deriving our sustenance from it. And maybe annoying it, slightly!"

" Okay, getting past the cover: *'everybody knows…a haiku has seventeen… syllables, three lines.'* See, that's not so tough. So what's the problem with the Boston Haiku Society? I've just looked through your book here, and it seems like for the most part, you guys don't know how to count."

"Depends on what you're counting."

"Syllables! Every language has them!"

"Well, yes and no. For example, that words "knows." How many syllables?"

"One, of course."

"Ah, in English, we count stresses as syllables. But how many different sound elements does it have?"

"Let's see…the 'n' sound, the long 'o' sound, and an 's' sound."

"The Japanese would count that as at least two, probably three, although separated a little differently: *NO-U-ZU.* Plus, they have a long, literary history of plugging expressions into that five-seven-five rhythm, in part derived from Chinese literature written in lines of five or seven characters. And in Japan, this rhythm even extends to making little catch phrases, public service announcements, like a sign I saw in Japan once:

Tobidasuna...kuruma wa kyu-u ni...tomarenai"

"Yeah, seventeen syllables, in five seven five. They put haiku on signs in Japan. Ah, what a poetic culture!"

"I would agree that they are, but as their success in engineering and business might suggest, they have a practical side, too. By the way, that 'verse' means, 'Don't jump out...cars cannot....quickly stop.' To warn kids from running into the streets, right? We might say, 'Look both ways!'"

"Kind of reminds me of the way rhyme was used in the old "Burma Shave" ads they used to place along the roads, like, 'Round the corners, take it slow. Let the little shavers grow: Burma Shave.'"

"Exactly. 5-7-5 rhythm has a deep resonance for Japanese. For English speakers, not so much."

"Well, in English, we rhyme and have meter. Why didn't the Japanese rhyme?"

"Too easy. Most Japanese words end in vowels. It would be boring. But we don't use rhyme in English haiku either. Why not? Well, Probably because of the time haiku started to spread in Europe and America. In the early twentieth century, English language poets were starting to move away from rhyme and even meter. Yeah, you get some scholars like Harold Henderson who used rhyme in their translations. But others, like R.H. Blyth didn't. Maybe his take on haiku as an expression of Zen was more along the lines of the times, the Beat fifties, the Eastern-mysticism- oriented sixties... So when non-Japanese really got into writing haiku, many of them free-verse poets, they went more for the essence of the form than its literary trappings."

"So it's all about Zen, seeing into the ultimate reality of things."

"There's a lot to be said for the Zen angle, and certainly, seventeenth century Japan and haiku's putative founder, Bashō, was steeped in it. But I like to think that if Zen has anything to teach, it goes to the heart of the human experience, and doesn't necessarily have to be wrapped up in a Buddhist package. The 'Zen' essence, if I had to take a stab at it, would be mindfulness, living in the moment, and seeing deep significance in a moment's worth of life. That's what English language haiku poets are going for, and I hope you can see that in the works in this book."

"So what makes haiku 'poems?' What puts them in the realm of literature rather than some sort of mystical expression?"

"In a sense, a haiku is just one person nudging another and saying, 'get a load of that.' But we don't usually have the convenience of having the world standing next to us to nudge when we experience something wonderful. That means we have to use that uniquely human device called language, and figure out a way to recreate our perception in the mind of another. Maybe some people do it with visual art, maybe you can do it through music. We choose to do it with just enough words. As few as possible. Too many, and the words start to get in the way of what we want to express. Too many metaphors, allusions, double-entendres, and then you get something else. A poem, not a haiku. Not that there's anything wrong with that, but…it's just not haiku.

"Yeah, but looking through this book, I see some literary devices. And actually, that's what I like about some of the haiku."

Sure. There's no hard line between a haiku and a poem in English.

There are some general rules though: it should be about a moment of existence, which usually means no past tense. No analogy or metaphor. But if the bottom line of the poem is more about experience than interpretation, you can sometimes get away with it. There's usually a place where you can break the haiku in two, after the first or second line. But you can write in one line and indicate the pause with a punctuation mark or grammatical pause. You know, the Japanese have actual words used for punctuation, like *ya* or *kana*! Cutting words, they're called. This division makes it possible to have complexity in such short verse. Some insist that a haiku should never be "just a sentence," and they've got a point. That break usually divides two different elements, two poles that must be bridged to "get" the haiku. Maybe that's why Bashō supposedly said that good haiku only show seventy, eighty percent of the subject. And if you can get away with fifty, then you've got something that people will never get tired of. Quite often, the real poetry is in the gaps of haiku.

> "Another thing I notice is all the seasonal references. Haiku seem to be 'spring this,' 'autumn that...'"

"Good observation. Yeah, for most Japanese, that's a non-negotiable. Seventeen syllables and the season word."

> "Isn't that kind of...cliché?"

"It certainly can be. But this is one aspect of haiku that is unique in literature, although we have little in our cultural background to help us here. So what's up with this fixation on the time of year? For starters, there's the sheer utility of the season word. In a poem as brief as the haiku, a season word is really a season *world*. Sometimes an acorn is not just an acorn. It's cooling nights, shorter days, turning leaves, streets filling with students and fields filling with grain. A Keats or even a Frost would go on for lines, feeling the need to fill in the details, no doubt delightfully. But in haiku, there's more power in suggestion than description."

" Of course, this is a lot easier for a traditional Japanese haiku poet. They can refer to their *saijiki*, or season word dictionaries, which list the allowable phrases, all neatly ordered by their seasonal appearance. There are thousands of phrases, classified into categories like weather, plants, animals, human activities, etc. Of course, we don't have anything like this, although there are some experimental English season word dictionaries…but I don't know of anyone who uses them with any regularity."

"Sounds awfully anal."

"Yeah, and even some contemporary Japanese poets have tried breaking away from this. Plus, I really don't think free-wheeling western poets could ever become *saijiki* junkies. Still, seasonal references are the intersection between time and the things of nature. I don't think it's an accident that haiku, the expression of a moment of experience, relies so heavily on the time of year: one precise moment in a broader 'moment.'"

"So no season, no haiku?"

"Oh no…there are plenty of insights you can have, even ones based on nature, that don't involve the seasons. I think there are very few absolute rules, except maybe the brevity, that can never be broken. Plus, the Japanese have another literary from, the *senryu*, that covers non-seasonal phenomenon. You can find some in this book. They mainly focus on human nature, more of what goes on inside us. Quite often, they're humorous, satirical. But not always. Some say that the most striking haiku contain strong elements of senryu. The upshot is, a good haiku poet uses everything at his or her disposal to craft the most effective verbal representation of experience. Seasons are strong…seasonings! And use of any other literary devices that other kinds of poets use: assonance, alliteration, a good ear for rhythm and the heft of a line…are all part of a good haiku poet's toolbox. The result is a poem that can be recited in one breath, one that sounds completely spontaneous, but is often the result of hours of work. One that, in both its topic and expression, helps us to share, as completely as possible, the experience of another human being. So read through the poems. Bring the images to life in your mind, and don't be afraid to make associations, fill in the empty spaces with your own experiences and imagination. Take a bite of the sun.

John Ziemba

Martha Akagi

Grinding black ink
Cherry branch
Blooming in a jar

Smell of mud
In the tree sap
The first tiny flies

Spring drizzle
Tiny fly explores pen
End to end

Child listening
Starling singing
In the bush

Sunbathers
Sprawled on the grassy slope
Dandelions

Rain soaked peony
Dropping petals
Into summer

Watering grass
Turning round and round
Rainbow circle

The salt wind
Billowing clouds
Sheets on the line

Long summer night
Pushing aside curtain
To catch a passing breeze

Visitors leaving
Creaking screen door
In the salt wind

Dawn
Glint of a spider web
On the pine bough

Out at sea
Spider with its filament
Sailing on an air current

In darkness
Morning star
Passing the pine

Moon
Hidden
In the clear blue sky

Handmade cradle
Mattress of milkweed fluff
For her teddy

Moonlight
In the teahouse
The shhhh of the brazier

Moonlight
Blue shadows
Crossing the snow

Snow powder
On the muddy slopes
Green shoots

Kaji Aso

on the lips
one sweet drop—
spring rain

spring snow
man goes running
steaming

do re fa la
spring rain hitting
all kinds of things

snowmelt:
crocus opens
still wet

very tiny
but I think I heard
crocus open

spring afternoon—
worm stretches out
worm shrinks

in the darkness
chasing after firefly
never catching it

ebb tide
new print
of a seagull

crescent moon
slightly shining
on the rose petal

swan buries her neck
into her body
dream floats on the pond

harvest moon
white breath
of the rat

harvest moon
spider, too
gazing at it quietly

cold autumn wind
lifts
the dragonfly's tail

open mouthed
biting the morning sun
winter carp

snow night
exquisite, but
monologue of radiator

new snow
footprint of a pigeon
footprint of a rat

snow melts...
how red and bright,
the feet of ducks

peony snow
dreaming of the far away
flower forest

Brad Bennett

streetlights…
my shadow and I
keep meeting

the rain slows
a pair of sneakers
slung on a wire

a boy rides circles
under the basketball hoop
high sun

another morning
a bagel rolls off
the counter

company for lunch
a dozen eggs knock
against the pot

a nail's shadow
on a weathered board
late afternoon

rusty lawn chair
the full moon reveals
its silver

wind scuffs
the marsh water...
a swallow's flight

winter pond
a swan's wake slips
under the ice

crows
calling out
the falling snow

fall into winter
the leaf and its shadow
frozen together

the pulse
of a grackle's wings
light rain

first snowfall...
shaking out vitamins
onto my palm

my feet
straddle the sun—
new swing set

school bus stop
maple leaf imprints
in the new sidewalk

summer evening
steamed broccoli with
a splash of lemon

autumn sun
a ginger cat snaps
at a moth

a drop of pond
at the end of a beak
setting sun

John Bergstrom

revere night:
hanging on corner, a teenager points the way
w/blue-lit cell-phone

cool summer breeze—a sparrow flying
between two shirtless fat men

birdsong after rain
toy dinos luminesce in green shade

Sunday morning wind black enamel suvs
reflect pretty girls

summer coolness—an upside down sparrow
shifts its feet for a grip

the hot afternoon—gutter water running
down into a dark hole

the heat of the sun, the whine of a weed
whacker and the smell of mint

after the heat wave, the sound of wind
chimes up and down the block

the September wind—trash and the shadows
of doves fly down the sidewalk

autumn—up on the ladder, painting the trim
as white as his beard

cold moon—one of the firemen takes off his
helmet—an old bald guy

winter sun—sparrow clinging to brick wall

bitter cold night, the flag standing out
straight, snapping hard

a second of sun-glare and the plane
disappears into distant clouds

reading the NEW DIRECTIONS ANTHOLOGY OF
CLASSICAL CHINESE
POETRY—*I came across T'ao Ch'ien's*
"Peach Blossom Spring" – a village of
"austere houses graced with fine fields and
lovely ponds," hidden from the turmoil of
the dynasties—i thought, the esplanade is
like that—"luxe, calme, et volupte"—only a
pipe dream, but:
cherry blossoms—from her father's
shoulders the child points this way and that

Shawna V. Carboni

a chipmunk sunning on a stone
lifts its nose
—hyacinth

eyeing the young squirrels,
eyeing the new birdfeeders

beach chairs
puddle with rain
June chill

wasp
hauling a blade of grass—
humid morning

the whole sky
in a cup of tea
—autumn picnic

round bellied squirrel
did you eat the harvest moon?

all heads lift to follow honking geese

Spring rain—
an earthworm traverses the garden path

evergreens
lashed to cartops—
advent

the puppy
catches snowflakes
forgetting to pee

ice skates
scraping against the back door
the pond still unfrozen

mending tears
needle in needle out
ignoring his complaints

a tiny toy dumptruck left on the bus...
tears at the dinner table

mowing lawns
the schoolboy
plans for an iPad

barefeet wiggling in mud ... late for summer school

widow...
a blue heron
on one leg

spring rain
the suck of webbed feet
in mud

first hearing aid
all the sounds
she didn't know she missed

Kenneth Elba Carrier

receding thunder...
one bullfrog
then another

star gazing...
all the chance meetings
of my ancestors

old palm reader
my life line
her longest yet

greased piglets—
the children
squealing too

crossing the hopscotch
two old women
avoid the lines

mother
not making sense
again today

old cat
catching birds
with her eyes

outside
the conference room window...
hummingbirds

business trip—
the crocuses
came and went

sunrise
the dragonfly
shifts its wings

from its wing
a glint of sunset...
resting dragonfly

morning fog
the crow's call
unanswered

arguing—
a deaf man grabs
the other's hands

snow flurries
separating two forests—
an old stone wall

killing frost—
all day a steady rain
of yellow leaves

blizzard day
extra brown sugar
on my oatmeal

winter sun
from the clothesline
bent towels

snowing
not snowing...
another log on the fire

Mike Cerone

beneath a gray cloud
the Moon
between night and day

sound of summer
at the bottom of the hill
bicycle turns

waving leaves
in the window
Teisho

discover home
in a dragon hall
ordination

How would Dogen hang
the TP roll?
zen bathroom

swaying trees
with the stillness of Buddha
wilderness zazen

shoulders
my arm just reaching
a father's hug

heads
above cubicle walls
layoffs today

a robin's stare
level with mine
next door rooftop

between concrete banks
the mill river rushes along
Monday morning commute

early morning
through the fog
sprinkler hiss

heat record
the fan drones over
tree whispers

tree frog
the sound of
the forest floor

silent flight
of dragonflies
dam noise

red traffic signal
starlings fly
from line to line

fresh bear sign
the flies rise up
to greet me

drying sleeping bag
instant oatmeal breakfast
on the trail

a step behind
the *Walden* quote
wildflowers

Andy Yen-Ting Chen

butterfly and I
cross paths
on the way to church

waiting at her doorstep
chocolate in one hand
Love Haiku the other

praying to God
wondering if
He prays too

hole in library parking
pool gathers
where sparrows splash about

little yellow dress
voice rises up and down
"seesaw seesaw"

sparrow plays
hopscotch board
one, two, three…fly

little girl
playing percussion
in her lap

phone phone phone
       txt
nobody's talking

door
ebbs
shut

voiceless
percussionist
of quarters, nickels, dimes

Summer embers
like firefly
for a moment

maple seeds
strewn about
so many dead tadpoles

Japanese Maple
dress-undressed
bare

brown dried leaf
raptured
awaiting butterfly

snow drop
ripples
through two still worlds

Halloween snow
Fall comes
dressed as Winter

single snowdrop
weighing eyelash
obscures my view

Snow upon snow
accumulates, compounds
heavenly silence

Sonia Coman

long walk
the birch bark
in early light

counting clouds
counting dreams
long flight home

closed moonflowers—
my watch still
on another time

daughter's letters
with the college logo—
ceaseless rain

dusty guest room
the blue shadow
of a rocking chair

lingering daylight—
numbered streets
toward the ocean

deserted windmill
the break in the wall
where a cloud lingers—

three pale moons
on the bus window—
highway through the city

high counter—
a wrinkled fist
full of candy

a pigeon lands
on the wooden horse
empty playground

observing
the tree's metal tag
a black bird

glowing sun
children
silently playing

silky mares—
the scent of fresh grass
carried by the wind

rustle of wings
a crow
uncovers the day moon

melting snow—
imprints of the rings
on their hands

medieval school—
revolving glass doors
reflect the frescos

amphitheater—
butterflies twirling
without an audience

a fallen leaf
out of the shadow
suddenly golden

Raffael de Gruttola

computer window
the face of
downtime

blues
harmonica player
comb with broken teeth

contact lens
finding it
with one eye

hot-walkers
the old thoroughbred
returns to its stall

walking alone
the filtered sounds
of the hototogisu

sleeping cats
on leaves of grass
the heat

in a field
of forget-me-nots
children fly kites

at sundown
in the stained glass window
shadow of a candle

driftwood in sand
strandings
echoing

high on an American elm
the hollow pecking
of the flicker

caged hamster
in candle glow
tent city

mime
changes his mask
...his mind

lost in the lights
the high fly ball
that never comes down

evening rush hour
the moon just another
headlight

winter wake
polar pup
on a floe

floating upriver
the garbage barge
with seagulls

the great horned owl
stops hooting
a murder of crows

deadened echoes
the white nose
of the little brown bat

Judson Evans

nesting season
the dead tree
sings

spring cursive
earthworm in the overturned
sod

country road's yellow lines
still visible
in the rubble

turning first
into the subway
blind man's cane

stopped school bus
all the years
studying patience

September cirrus
hot tar
cooling on the roof

studly dog-walker
I let my dog
check out his

near the playground
the old tree buds
with surveillance cameras

tutus and beads
carnival's
first responders

maple leaf caught
in the pine bonsai
one season touches another

piano four hands
watching who gets
the pedal

excited to see me
cell phone glows
through his pocket

10. *Gamelan*

First the limestone, itself, as a medium of sound, its resonance
and concussive timbres. There is a technical term
for the xylophone of these stones under foot… Crunch isn't it;
more resistant, a vibration angling off, as the piece I picked up and swung
in my left hand tapped against the plastic stay on my backpack. *Phonolithic.*
A gamelan of instruments struck with sensitive mallets. The way the wind
on Ventoux cancel out all sound, scrapes the surface clean, so when it briefly stops,
vibrations are coaxed out- the cyclists' whir of spokes, the motorcycle roar,
our own breathing…

on Ventoux/ the thunder of a jet/ muted in a fountain

Gwenn Gurnack

rain from the west
sifts through the porch screen—
the evening cool

pock
of tennis balls—
the heat

lake trout rising
to fireflies
among the stars

window flung wide—
this everyday mind I thought was mine
is Mind

dad flicks a fly
from grandpa's hand—
open casket

red oak leaf
on the wind
on its own

boink
of an aluminum bat...
red sky

empty fairgrounds—
tent peg holes
half filled

in pre-dawn light
an empty rowboat
trailing oars

evening star...
the cornhusker
brushes back her hair

in the line not waiting—being

head over heels
she leaves a stupid message
on his smart phone

vaulted stone cathedral—
candle by candle
darkness to light

snowflakes
on my scarf
turning into wool

rings
in a felled oak...
snow on snow on snow

still watching me
with her knowing look—
my childhood doll

ripping wind
snaps the flags
U. N. Plaza

her texted outrage
sent
with a well placed tap

Kay Higuchi

dream for a green frog
three turns
in the tuck position

pulse
of a hydrangea vein
a raindrop tumbles

summer moon
in her womb
~ripples~

dying father
wants a white peach
winter light

the sun
in the tip of icicle
lingers

still night
the silence of a cricket
perfectly clear

Moldavian Danube

Despite my doubts, my husband put his belongings in the trunk when the beautiful Moldavian woman opened it. It means that he'll lose all his stuff if they become wolves. And now, the woman and her husband, who is driving his car to the border between Romania and Moldova, insists on seeing their grandparents and eating their soup. I look at my husband desperately. He looks pale and desperate too. We refuse politely without showing our desperation. He doesn't stop the car. We are prisoners in the car. Soon we'll be given soup with a sleeping drug and robbed of everything.......Ahhhhhhhh!

When we met their grandparents, we were convinced of our safety. They looked honest. It was chicken noodle soup. We ate fresh tomatoes and cucumbers instead of soup (we don't eat meat usually) and homemade bread. They live in a beautiful Moldavian house which was used by head officers of the Nazi occupation forces during the war. They engage in farming and raising chickens.

A quiet and pastoral place.

Finally we feel we are alive.

pitch-dark night of spring
the only certainty
the sound of my water

young bamboo shoot—

from the ground

under the ground

ceaseless snow~

hesitating to say

"sorry"

Donald Kelly

brilliant sun
the new life
of a tiny red dragonfly

pouring rain
the smelt netter
wades under the bridge

window washers
play out their ropes
across summer clouds

the lovers
driving on a rainy night
kiss at the stop sign

July heat
from the dripping moss
I bathe my face

after the August rains
the big plane tree
heavy and still

the earth
a constant sound
unheard

among the mosses
and hemlock roots—
white Indian pipes

the golden fur
of the old muskrat
dead in the ditch

New wallet—
she finds a place for
a folded check

grey autumn sky—
a rabbit chews
a fallen pear

autumn morning—
garden stone
cool in my palm

Autumn deepens—
wanting to start
on the mission trail

snowy day—
the TV chef
whips up a meringue

winter dusk—
the satyr's grim face
on the garden bench

steam radiators
gurgle
room to room

winter seclusion—
the last slice of bread
thrown out to the crows

remaining snow—
you know
where north is

Karen Klein

everywhere yellow
the wildness
of forsythia

wheels
out of alignment
March heat wave

against the darkness
a solitary star's
radiance

March Wind
checking its directions
for his ashes

hospital corridor
someone calling
for her mother

tomato blight
rethinking
summer's menus

going home
the rusted metal
of old bridges

grandma's heavy rouge
tree rings concealed
beneath the bark

one head
for the electric toothbrush
is enough now

retiree's garden
blue hydrangea blossoms
fading

vacant patio chairs
the staccato of acorns
dropping

low slant
of the late afternoon sun
missing you

early darkness
still too early
to drink

afternoon sky
18 month old
finds the moon

winter sun
the smile on my ex-
husband's face

tossing
turning
the longest night

blizzard
wishing I had made
that soup

icicle
becomes a prism
Winter Solstice

Jeannie Martin

how different
the sound of rain
new apartment

reading alone
the ant won't shake
off the page

no path
one stone leads
to another

gathered around
the bird feeder
lawn chairs

no need
for a pond
day lily

just when
things seemed solid
Jupiter

shoreline
beyond the lighthouse
beyond the moon

evening sail
a sudden swell
of stars

mountain hike
I try to keep pace
with myself

always a little
uneven—
peace vigil circle

old woman
her bent
smile

deathwatch
how deliberate
making the tea

New Year's Day
eating an apple
core and all

lasts even longer
faded
cherry blossom

easter eve
the deep silence
of stars

old cemetery
the path
a little too narrow

missing you
a cloud
of dragonflies

deep inside
the fog
the fog

Lauren Mayhew

shooting star
my wish for
an unhurried life

long stretch
of interstate highway—
smooth jazz

hotel room
on the pillow, a hair
longer than mine

beach cottage
the musty smell
of old novels

garage sale
a leaf spins onto
the stack of 45s

swing and a miss
the radio announcer's voice
drowns out the rain

wet fallen leaves
again he evades
my question

forgiveness
neatly folding
his underwear

September dusk
fading light
through monarch wings

first cold day
the cat kneads
a patch of sunlight

purple hues
in her silver hair
autumn twilight

starless night
the small comfort
of tree lights

deep winter
the smell of coconut
from my lip balm

new year
on the salon floor
last year's split ends

city bus
a diversity
of ring tones

first warm day
the hum
of Harleys

spring breeze
a wisp of hair
escapes her burka

blue heron
perfectly still
the birdwatcher

Paul Mena

overcast night—
searching for
the Hunter's Moon

between skyscrapers
shadows with wings

All Soul's Day—
an old man
feeding sparrows

frost warning—
all alone
together

cold snap—
staring at
strike three

suburban gridlock—
two Mercedes
lock horns

searching for words
an acorn falls

fading and brittle
his crayon portrait
of me

dive bar—
a regular claims
to recognize me

on the back
of a rejection letter
my next haiku

Election week—
the flag hangs
limply

falling temperatures—
these whispering
pines

Day of the Dead—
broken tree limbs
in the road

fair-weather clouds—
an ultrasound
of my next grandchild

first snow—
an almost
perfect shave

so in love
with that song
I miss my exit

slow blues—
the bass player
yawns

full moon—
an empty pint
of ice cream

June Moreau

shaping itself on the pond   the spring wind

a tuft of fur
caught in the fence
where the groundhog scrambled under

a reluctant shadow
tags after him—
the groundhog

loosening the stars
and me with them
the waterfall

lighting a lamp
to thread a needle
the mosquito's voice

squinting my ears
to hear it
the hummingbird's voice

I think the sky
is thinking
and clouds are thoughts

my child's tears
how small they are
the faraway stars

bitter cold
only the snowman
has a smile

standing by the pond
skates over his shoulder—
the snowman

winter stillness
I can hear the sounds
of moving clouds

the winter wind
in the white pines—
my only song

Winter Solstice—
go out of doors
and see time stand still
on the moon's
silvery doorstep

having homemade donuts
flavored with nutmeg
for breakfast
and outside my window
a wren is singing

I vote
for the red apple
on the windowsill
with the winter sun
shining on it

take three pebbles
of shining quartz,
the evening song of a flute
multiply them
by the flight of a plover

Brett Peruzzi

egret fishing
the tide rises
with the morning sun

tracing the canyon wall
above the petroglyphs
a raven's shadow

Empty storefront—
YES WE'RE OPEN sign
curling at the edges

boarded up general store
the rusted gas pump
stopped at $2.65

Gathering the day's trash
the streetsweeper
pauses with the sports section

Ebb tide
a harbor seal's call
echoes across the cove

Cajun musician
squeezing the bayou
out of his accordion

Song about hard times
the bluesman's gold tooth
flashes with each grimace

endless meeting
the VP whose hair
never moves

Autumn wind—
the rattling
of a lone cornstalk

Identifying
his wife's corpse
her watch still ticking

Afternoon beer joint—
the pinball machine's
last bell fades out

behind the police station
the mockingbird's
siren song

carnival midway
the missing tooth
in the barker's smile

break in the conversation
a few bars of jazz piano
fill the silence

A car's dragging muffler
throws a trail of sparks
autumn night

Late evening
a bottle rolls up and down
the empty subway car

A phoebe's cry—
river water drips
from the stilled canoe paddle

Larry Rungren

first day of spring
last year's leaves
scatter in the wind

early spring morning
a sparrow bathes itself
in snowmelt

the way raindrops
angle into the bay
spring rain

spring dusk—
the place where a stone
was pulled from the ground

3:00 AM
the shadow of the house
beneath the full moon

morning train
the steady clack
of a laptop's keys

concert over
the note the wind sounds
in the empty band shell

summer flies—
the slow swat
of a cow's tail

dog day night
turning my pillow
to the cool side

October sun—
the buzz of bees
around the cider press

from which window
the sound of someone crying
November dusk

a night
without dreams
winter rain

bitter night
the new moon's
passing darkness

deserted siding
snowflakes flutter
among the empty boxcars

deer tracks
heading off into the woods
snow moon

the fire's warmth
burns itself out
short winter afternoon

drawing my arms
close around myself
winter rain

late winter morning
from the bare field
smell of the earth

Reiko Seymour

しだれ桜風もなく散る友逝きて

> Weeping cherries
> Falling without wind
> Gone is my friend

雪解けに胸ふくらます駒鳥かな

> Spring thaw
> A robin's chest
> All puffed up

炎天下隠れる影なき白い道

> Scorching sun
> No shade to hide
> A parched road

青紫蘇とネギとゴマで喰う絹豆腐

> Green shiso
> Scallion and sesame seeds
> On silken tofu

釣り人の一人佇む麦わら帽

> A lone angler
> Stands still
> A straw hat

フンコロガシゾウのフンまるめて嫁をとる

> A dung beetle
> Rolling, rolling elephant dung
> Into the honeymoon chamber

夜道行く十五夜の月伴にして

A night's journey
A harvest moon
Shines my way

振り向けば遠くの空に秋去りぬ

Looking back
In a distant sky
The Autumn is gone

獅子舞の囃子にぎやか今父母のなき

The Lion Dance
With festive music
Gone are my parents

音もなく雪ふり降りる彼の誕生日

Not a sound
Snowflakes swirling
On his birthday

草むらに動かぬチーター風揺れる

Inside the dry grass
A cheetah sits still
Weeds sway in the wind

待ちきれず植えたパンジー雪の下

Pity on pansies
Fooled by warm air
Under the snow

夕暮れ沼ビーバー家族の夕餉どき

Marsh at dusk
Sounds of supper
Of a beaver family

古希の春城山の桜遠くなり

70th spring
Cherry blossoms at the castle
Far away

浅黄色枝を伸ばして命満つ

Fresh green leaves
Stretching to the sky
Full of life

トリリアム深山に一人誰を待つ

Trillium
Alone in the mountain
Waiting for someone?

91

Tom Seymour

Breeze across the pond
Afar the mountains linger—
Long breath of summer

Still white clouds above
Undulate beneath my feet
Hanging off the pier

Eyes so intense
Mind struggling for words—
A child not yet two

Grandchildren gone
Only the birds are noisy
Our house so quiet

Through a basement window
Lordly chipmunk perched on tire
Surveys his domain

Red loafers for him
Canvas High Tops for Francis
New Bishop of Rome

A bird's
Fast-fading footprints
Deepen snow's silence

Mounds of grey moguls
Metamorphose at leisure~
Mud season

Our breakfast nook tree
With buds still in waiting
Nostalgia for spring

Spring sunlight glistens
On countertops warm—
Ladybugs convene

Richard St Clair

the shrouded moon
no mouth
no eyes

feather
on the sidewalk
pointing east

a worm
in two pieces
squirming

winter surf
a starfish
mounting a mussel

winter lilac leaves
little handfuls
of snow

after
the colonoscopy
cold drizzle

again the heat
the robin's
open beak

a sunray
touching
her wrinkled nightie

finding
a child's hand
nightfall in Aleppo

the handyman
after all these years
so many stories

sixty-sixth birthday
hair everywhere
but my head

again
the humid heat
chattering sparrows

RAINBOW SEQUENCE

a list
of unkept promises
the rainbow's end

twilight daydream
the rainbow
still aglow

half a rainbow
dissolving
into dark clouds

the rainbow
in dusky twilight
her final breath

rainshine
in the west
double rainbow

a faint rainbow
I hear and answer
buddha's call

Walter Valeri

sea-gull
open wings on the asphalt
another ocean

red stain
on the wall the mosquito
another's blood

on the dusty window
of a passing car
my name

then suddenly: I stole
years ago one of your lines—
did you need it?

in the deepest forest
step by step
the fruits of the mind

dead sparrow
on a flower-bed
without feathers

the cardinal quits
untouchable
the swinging branch

dance of the spider
on the exhausted insect
burst of gunfire

under the stars
the chasm resurfaces
from frozen grass

hurricane floods
in the valley of death
sprouts and twigs reborn

a shade of two ears
amid the lettuce
the happy herbivore

behind the wall of the churchyard
songs of the blackbird
as if he never left

on the young shoulders
weeps the old widow
athlete without hope

creaking from the branch
in the grasp of the wind
restless night

rain and hailstones
on the gold of natur
leaves of the last day

yellow blaring leaves
thousands fall
limit of the memory

nightly gusts
elevate for a while
columns of leaves

March sun
the snow melts
where the brook flees

Zinovy Vayman

in between death
and the return to death
sweet snow

expanse of the sea
the white seagull
so black at sunrise

Ars Longa
Vita Brevis
gladiolus

Moscow subway ride
the stray dog and I
rocking in sync

atop the fence shadow
the cat's shadow
gazing at me

snowed in…
the givens
of my long life

in between whitecaps
the bands of dark night
the bands of sunset

opposite window
the snow in the distant one
descends slower

gated community:
the old pond had vanished
from the new map

City Lights Bookstore
someone else's fart
smells like mine

small gate opens...
the cypress shadow jumps
into her yard

spacious bedroom
the inaudible mosquito
so tender, so slow

Moscow Book Festival

The Festival compound was located on the Crimean Avenue and all its pavilions were named after the legendary localities on the remarkable peninsula on the Black Sea. The central one was a cafeteria 'Chufut Kale."

I was hanging out choosing people to poll them for the meaning of these two words. Nobody knew. I gleefully informed them—"The Jewish Fortress."

After all, I was in an anti-Semitic country and the innocent ignorance of the organizers amused me greatly. Not a clue. Not a clue, *shmegegge*.

All of a sudden I noticed a young Hebrew capped with a yarmulke. And the chap gave the correct reply! How come he knows the Turkic word? Why is he here on Shabbes? Who is he? Why is he here?

Ten minutes later I found him sitting among a discussion panel on the recent developments in Russian language bending slightly under the victorious onslaught from the Germanic West. He talked about the eyes of a blogger soaking up language mutations; he mentioned grammar Nazis, new lexicons and emerging jargons. Nosik is his name. Ah, Nosik, Remnik, Gopnik, Gorelik, Gorali,...Linor Goralik (of Moscow via Israel via Ukraine) announced, "Language is a living organism." The quick Hebrew mind Kaganov informed us about the points of bifurcation and homonyms. He insisted on the legalization of expletives and started to swear elegantly.

The moderator, Maxim Krongauz (Crown House)—a great German last name for an Ashkenazi Israelite—was disseminating his observations about the multilingualism of blogs and the taboos overheating the language matrix. So many devils in so many details...I speak and write with a Russian accent. Still, am I losing my mother tongue? My grandmother's tongue was Lithuanian Yiddish but my mother does not use it anymore. And our family vernacular is dissipating already.

Two young panelists—Russian Russians—chimed in with their notions that written languages were not suitable for humans and texts were bound to end. They commented on the pulverization of language and the survivability of new words. They spotlighted the hybridization of the Japanese and Russian tongues via cartoons... Ah, music to my haikai ears...

But in the next instant I overheard my own, a bit alien, voice: "We are sitting in Russia, in Russia, in Moscow; we are well into the 21st century. Why are so many Jews here on a panel discussing the language of Russians? Eighty percent! What's going on?" The mostly Russian audience burst into the loudest laughter.

Linor stared at me while Krongauz rose up searching for words, "Well, this is the deal now. We do not talk here about curses and Jews, OK?"

**July heat
my mom complains about
sex with my father**

John Ziemba

into the March wind
the tilt
of the tombstone

its little mouth
receiving the April rain
wine bottle

trying to forget—
a field of grass
in first seed

city puddle
butts
and buds

thunderbolt—
the white agitation
of the pansies

inside the breaker
a tunnel of light
is crushed

trying to converge…
all the raindrop rings
in all the puddles

alone in the blackout
the weight
of the dead batteries

house spider
knows
this isn't really my house either

red
inside red
inside red—
pomegranate

the heft of an apple
disappears
as I eat it

middle-aged
I eat around
the apple's bruises

autumn night...
the weight of it
on every leaf

suburban scarecrow—
birdfeeder
in each hand

chasing
a plastic bag,
a diversity of leaves

icicles
straight
on the crooked shed

below zero
the sincere face
of the dead possum

frozen snow
less and less a thing of the sky
more and more a thing of the earth

Old Friends

Drops of rain
washing themselves
in the birdbath

Glenn Gustafson

the barefoot girl
catches a milkweed
lets it go

Steven Small

The doctor shakes her head
for a moment
silence

David Schuster

fog over the lake
in the fisherman's boat
glimmering of a lantern

Balazs Kosaras

knife through the apple
smell of the orchard
hands full of stars

Sarah Jensen

from the coiled
   garden hose
      last
     drops
      of
      sun

Rich Youmans

another tear
in the butterfly's wing—
lingering autumn light

Marilyn Murphy

the pallbearers
last year's acorns
crunch underfoot

Keith Heiberg

will you still be here
in spring—
     brown leaf

        Brenda Soyer

sunlit clouds
now in every crack
of stone Buddha

        Bruce Ross

Walden Pond
in its original blue...
shining autumn leaves

        Tadashi Kondo

Boston Marathon:
April 15th, 2013

Some haiku in response to the tragic terror bombing
of the Boston Marathon.

BOSTON MARATHON
118th running…
    Flags at half mast

                Raffael de Gruttola

praise be to those
running into the fray
not away

                Gwenn Gurnack

morning after
the bombing
birdsong

                Lauren Mayhew

April shadows…
the chalk outlines
of little children

John Ziemba

only the wrap of silver foil
between exhilaration
and panic

Judson Evans

a body like Hercules
no one will bury
golden gloves*

Judson Evans

*The mother of the bombing suspects described her older son Tamerlan Tsarnaev as "having the body of Hercules." After the bombing there was much conflict and public recrimination about burying his body.

after the bombing
the subway train
skips a stop

Brad Bennett

The Members of the Boston Haiku Society

Martha Rice Akagi

Martha Rice Akagi is an artist educator from New England who seeks the beauty in life with haiku, paint and music. She studied with Kaji Aso for many years. With sincere thanks to Boston Haiku society poets for their critiques, she looks forward to their support in her efforts to use the short form haiga.

Kaji Aso 麻生花児

Kaji Aso (1935 - 2006) was a painter, poet, philosopher, teacher, tenor, marathoner, and river adventurer, and founder and director of the Kaji Aso Studio, the home of the Boston Haiku Society. From his unique perspective, he strove to bridge the gap between East and West and tirelessly sought out universal value in all the many arts he pursued. A graduate of Tokyo University School of Art, he first came to the U.S. in 1967 to become a professor of Art at the Boston Museum of Fine Arts School. Soon after, his students pressed him to establish his own school and began to meet regularly at an apartment on St Stephen Street. The Studio grew over the years, eventually comandeering the entire building and incorporating workshops in painting, drawing, ceramics, poetry, Japanese calligraphy, tea ceremony and music. The Kaji Aso Studio soon became well-known in Boston for its gallery openings, concerts, and rowdy Octopus Parties. Mr Aso led groups of artists in annual runnings of the Boston Marathon and canoe/kayak trips down rivers such as the Hudson, Mississippi, Shinano (Japan), Seine, Volga, Nile and Tajo (Spain and Portugal). The essence of his philosophy was that life does not come from art—art comes from life. He encouraged his students to approach their themes from a variety of perspectives—writing haiku was often an integral part of his instruction to painters. Writers often found themselves running miles and miles through snowy nights, and musicians honed their ears on the gurglings of great rivers. He was a source of constant guidance and inspiration to the Boston Haiku Society and his irreverent humor, imagination, and indomitable love of life are deeply missed.

Brad Bennett

Brad Bennett teaches elementary school in the Boston area and has taught haiku to children for almost twenty years. He has also led haiku walks for adults at the Great Meadows National Wildlife Refuge in Concord, MA. Brad's haiku and senryu have been published in a variety of print and online journals and magazines. Some of his poems have also won awards in haiku contests. Brad loves to walk in local conservation areas, Audubon sanctuaries, wildlife refuges, national parks, and Japanese gardens to find haiku inspiration. The "way of haiku" helps him get out of his head and into the world!

113

John Bergstrom

John (almost certainly) first ran into the idea of haiku way back in the 60's, the way they were imbedded in the writings of Jack Kerouac – and there was Ferlinghetti's "Back Roads to Far Places", and so on – then at some point he actually studied them at a weekend retreat at Zen Mountain Monastery with Clark Strand – and then got involved with the Boston Haiku Society for some years – he hasn't been able to get to meetings lately, but he still writes from time to time: "must be a poet – waiting for a cloud to drift behind the full moon."

Shawna V Carboni

Shawna V Carboni has been writing haiku and member of BHS since 2011. Having written poetry for many years, she is drawn to haiku precisely because it requires the poet not only to attend to nuances in nature and life, but then to distill the essence of a particular moment and situation—in only a few words—to give the reader an experience, a felt-sense of that moment and its meaning. Such is the challenge and delight of writing haiku and senyru.

Kenneth Elba Carrier

Kenneth Elba Carrier (Ken) discovered the beauty of haikus and senryu in 2006, and he became a member of the Boston Haiku Society that same year. Since then he has been fascinated with the ability of these seemingly simple collections of the perfect handful of words to elegantly convey so many emotions and ideas. Ken has published numerous haiku and senryu and won awards from the Boston Haiku Society and The Haiku Society of America. Ken works as a consultant to the medical product industry and also operates a company in which he visits elementary schools to teach science programs. He is an outdoor enthusiast and enjoys hiking, kayaking, fishing, and organic gardening.

Mike Cerone

Mike Cerone, lives in Arlington, MA and is a father of a teenage son. He pays the rent as an IT professional, enjoys being in the mountains of NH and practices Zen at Greater Boston Zen Center (part of Boundless Way Zen). He picked up haiku about two years ago in part to satisfy his long love of writing and also as part of his Zen practice. This haiku practice has brought many good and interesting things in his practice and experience of life, a new to open up to the world and new friends.

Yen Ting (Andy) Chen

Andy is a teacher and life long learner. He was introduced to haiku as a child by a kind student-teacher in 4th grade and rediscovered his love for poetry and the form about seven, eight years ago. He loves sharing his work with fellow enthusiasts, reading haiku from masters of all eras and ages, and writing and refining his work while sharpening his haiku eyes and haiku mind. "Writing is painting with words; the imagination is the canvas."

Sonia Coman

Sonia received her B.A. in 2011 in Art History with a Secondary Field in Studio Art from Harvard University (Magna cum Laude, Phi Beta Kappa). She worked as a student docent for the Harvard Art Museums and as a curatorial intern in the Department of Paintings at the Louvre Museum in Paris. Since starting her Ph. D. program in Art History at Columbia University, Sonia received her Master of Arts (2012) and Master of Philosophy (2014) degrees, conducted research in Paris, and wrote reviews of contemporary art for a New York-based magazine. Her doctoral research focuses on the influence of Japanese ceramics on nineteenth-century French art. Sonia is an active member of the core team of C.A.E.S.A.R., a think-tank of young experts in a variety of fields whose aim is the sustainable development of Romania. She is also an avid reader and writer of poetry and particularly of haiku, tanka, and renku.

Raffael de Gruttola

Past President and Treasurer of the Haiku Society of America. Presently, 2nd Vice President of the Tanka and Haiku Society of America. A founding member of the Boston Haiku Society in 1988 and a recent member of the Alewife Brook Haiku Group. Helped in the organization of two renku groups: the Renkubluz Haiku Group and the Immature Green Heron Group. Was the main coordinator of the Haiku North America Conference of Boston in 2001. Mr. de Gruttola has been writing haiku since the early seventies and his haiku have appeared in all the main haiku magazines in the USA, Canada, and throughout Europe and Japan. He also edited the Boston Haiku News from 1990 to 2010 and recently **A *Life in Haiku: The Haiku of Nick Virgilio*** from Turtle Light Press. He has lectured on haiku in major conferences in the US and Europe and has been invited on three occasions to Japan to participate in Renku Conferences.

115

Judson Evans

Judson Evans is Director of Liberal Arts at The Boston Conservatory where he teaches a set of Poetry Workshops and Humanities electives. In fall 2007, he was chosen by John Yau as an Emerging Poet by the *Academy of America Poetry*. He has published a haibun chapbook, *Mortal Coil* with Leap Press and continues to write and publish both Japanese-based forms and contemporary lyric poetry (and find a cross-pollination between the two.)

Gwenn Gurnack

A life-long poet and author of two published poetry books, I discovered my true poetic voice just under four years ago. I awakened one morning with a lovely poem in my thought, wrote it down, and realized that it contained seventeen syllables. "Could this be a haiku?" I asked myself. The rest is history. Since that day, I have become an active member of the Boston Haiku Society and appeared in the BHS Monthly News an average of four times per issue, taken weekly haiku lessons with John Ziemba of Kaji Aso Studio, read everything I could find about the history and how-to of haiku, studied the works of the Masters, and devoured every haiku anthology in print. I have written over four thousand haiku and senryu during these fast-flying months, which has afforded me little time for marketing, entering contests, and self promotion. I do have a large mailing list, and as you will see, have been regularly published in excellent journals and have won some very respectable contests. B.A. Chatham University, Pittsburgh, PA. Major: Music, piano concentration. Minors: English and Psychology. Graduate work in business administration, consciousness raising, communication skills. Present occupations: poet (a five-mile walk around Boston rain or shine per day experiencing the city--gathering information for and writing haiku and senryu); piano teacher and full-time substitute piano teacher at the Community Music Center of Boston; performer at occasional piano gigs; student of metaphysics; spiritual healer; and frequently published poet in The Christian Science Journal and The Christian Science Sentinel.

Kay Higuchi

Born in Tokyo. Grew up with popular TV show series in 1960's and 1970's, "Laramie," "Lassie," "Bewitched," "Mission Impossible" and "Star Trek." At age 18, she was fascinated with Kumiko Torikai, a simultaneous interpreter. Graduated Sakura no Seibo Junior College where she met Sister Joan Giroux, who is the author of *The Haiku Form*. Resident of Boston since 2002. A member of the BHS and Gendai Haiku Internet Kukai in Japan.

Donald Kelly

Donald Kelly: founding member of the Boston Haiku Society in 1988. His interest in archeology and especially rock art took him after leaving Boston, to different archeological sites throughout the United States. In particular Joshua Tree National Park, Hickison Summit in Nevada; Chaco Canyon; The Great Serpent in Adams County, Ohio; and Mount Hood in Portland, Oregon, to mention just a few. Donald died of a lung disorder called sarcoid at home on October 8th in Chicago. One of his last haiku was: *cranes bring good luck / they say.../ for the rest of the week I'm ill."* Donald was in his mid forties at his passing. (Information on his travels was sent to Raffael de Gruttola through a long correspondence between them.)

Karen Klein

Karen Klein writes haiku/senryu and lyric poems. Her haiku/senryu have been published in numerous contemporary haiku periodicals, in three anthologies(*Red Moon, Basho, American Haibun and Haiga*),in two chapbooks from the Boston Haiku Society, in *Haiku: Poetry Ancient & Modern*, ed. J. Hardy and in Bruce Ross, *How to Haiku*. Her lyric poems were published online in *the drunkenboat* and *Scoutcambridge*. A modern dancer, she is a member of Prometheus Dance Elders Ensemble and also performs with Across the Ages Dance. Her sculptures are shown at Galatea Fine Art and she is a member of New England Sculptors and Studios Without Walls.

Jeannie Martin

Jeannie Martin has been writing and teaching haiku for the past 15 years. The author of several chapbooks, her work has also been published in a number of journals and anthologies. Her book, Clear Water: a haiku invitation into our luminous, sacred world was published in 2013 by Red Moon Publications in Oklahoma City. She is a member of the Boston Haiku Society and the Alewife Brook Haiku group.

Lauren Mayhew

Lauren Mayhew lives in Somerville, MA. Her main sources of creative inspiration are her urban neighborhood, time spent in the Berkshire Mountains and on outer Cape Cod, her relationship with her husband, and her ten-year old cat. Her haiku and tanka awards include: Special Mention, The Heron's Nest Reader's Choice Awards for 2012; Runner Up, The Haiku Calendar Competition (2013 and 2014); and Honorable Mention, Tanka Society of America International Contest (2013). When she is not writing poetry, Lauren is a wellness coach, a journal writing instructor, and yogini.

Paul Mena

Paul David Mena has been writing haiku since 1992, has written three chapbooks and is currently a member of numerous on-line haiku communities. He has contributed to Moongarlic, Frogpond, Modern Haiku, The Heron's Nest and Brussels Sprout, but more recently can be found on Twitter, where he attempts to post at least one new haiku every day. He has worked in the Computer industry for over 30 years and has lived in the Boston area since 1996. He is father to five children, seven grandchildren, and one cantankerous dog.

June Moreau

"I have always had an affinity for small things and the deep feelings they create—thus tanka and haiku are a natural for me." June lives and writes in Lexington, Massachusetts.

Brett Peruzzi

Brett Peruzzi, of Framingham, MA, has been writing and publishing haiku and related poetry forms for over 25 years. For more than a decade he has been writing and performing renku as part of the Metro West Renku Association, which created the blue notes renku form, an Americanized variation based on the twelve bar blues music form. He has also published longer free verse poems in many literary journals and currently writing a book-length memoir.

Larry Rungren

First introduced to the form through the books of R. H. Blyth, Lawrence Rungren has been writing haiku since the 1970s. He grew up in Illinois, spent several years in Wisconsin, and has lived in the Boston area since 1983. He was one of the founders of the Boston Haiku Society in the late 1980s and was co-editor of the BHS's first member anthology, *the ant's afternoon*. He is also editor of the twice-yearly regional journal, The Nor'Easter, which has published the work of many of New England's haiku poets.

Reiko Seymour

I was born and educated in Matsuyama, Ehime, Japan. Although Matsuyama produced many literary people, including Masaoka Shiki, I first became interested in Haiku after I moved to the US with my American husband and joined BHS, about a year and a half ago. I have been working as a simultaneous interpreter both in Tokyo and the US for the last 30 years.

Tom Seymour

Tom Seymour was born in Boston, raised in Connecticut, and educated at Dartmouth College, B.A. Government, and the University of Michigan, M.A. Japanese Studies. I spent over three decades living in Japan: first went in 1964 for two years serving in the US Marine Corps, subsequently as a graduate student (when I married my Japanese wife). I joined the Boston Haiku Society in the spring of 2012.

Richard St Clair

Richard St. Clair (b. 1946) has been writing haiku for twenty years. A native of North Dakota, he has lived most of his life in New England. His doctorate from Harvard is in music composition, an endeavor which has resulted in over one hundred "modern classical" musical compositions in most major genres such as symphony, solo sonatas, choral music and string quartets among others. In addition to haiku he is also a tanka enthusiast and more recently has become involved in renku composition. His haiku, renku and tanka have been published in major print journals and online.

Walter Valeri

Walter Valeri, Master's of Performing Arts, ART/MAXT Institute at Harvard University, is a distinguished poet, playwright, translator, and scholar. His collection of poetry, *Canzone dell'amante infelice* (Guanda) was awarded Italy's national literary prize, the Mondello. He worked for 15 years as personal assistant with the Nobel Prize in Literature Dario Fo, and Franca Rame.

Valeri has edited a Fo's standard sourcebook, *Fabulazzo* (KAOS), and is the author of various essays, including *Franca Rame, A Woman on Stage* (Perdue University Press), *An Actor's Theater* (Southern Illinois University Press). An anthology of his poems, *Deliri fragili*, was published in 2006 (Besa Editrice). He translated in Italian several plays and literary works, among the others: *Knepp* and *Krinsky* by Jorge Goldenberg, *Nobody Dies on Friday* by Robert Brustein, *Adramelech* by Valére Novarina, *A German Requiem* by James Fenton, and *Pebbles from My Skull* by Stuard Hood. Valeri uses haiku as a bridge between Italian and American sensibilities and draws strength from both. He continues to be active in Italy as artistic director of the International Poetry Summer Festival *Il Porto dei Poeti*.

Zinovy Vayman

Zinovy Vayman, Russian Jew, composes haiku in English, Russian and Hebrew, sometimes, successfully. He is haibun editor of Simply Haiku, The Art of Haiku magazine. He attempts to write rhymed verses in Russian. Recently he won The International Haiku contest in Moscow with: *if everything/were so puerile—/the bluebell*

John Ziemba

John Ziemba was born in Rochester, New York and began living in Boston in 1978, where besides a brief stint in Pittsburgh to get a Masters in Asian literature and a longer stint in Japan teaching English, he has been ever since. He became a member of the Kaji Aso Studio in 1982, leading poetry, haiku and renku workshops and dabbling in calligraphy every now and then. He currently is teaching international students English, writing haiku, poetry and short stories, and is occasional successful in keeping out of trouble.

CREDITS

Brad Bennett: "streetlights" from Frogpond 36:2 (13); "the rain slows" from Modern Haiku 44:3 (13); "company for lunch" Second Prize, Kaji Aso Studio International Contest (13); "a nail's shadow" from bottle rockets 28 (13); "rusty lawn chair" Honorable Mention, Autumn Moon Haiku Contest, Bangor Haiku Group (13); "wind scuffs" from The Nor'Easter 18:2 (13); "crows" from The Nor'Easter 18:1 (13); "fall into winter" from Acorn 30 (13); "the pulse" from The Nor'Easter 18:2 (13); "first snowfall..." from bottle rockets 30 (14); "a drop of pond" Heron's Nest Award Runner Up from The Heron's Nest 13:2 (11). All others by permission of the author.

Kenneth Elba Carrier: "receding thunder" first prize in Kaji Aso Studio Haiku Contest (10); "star gazing" third prize in Kusamakura Haiku Contest (07); "old palm reader" honorable mention in HAS Brady Senryu Contest (08); "greased piglets" from bottlerockets Fairs Anthology (07); "crossing the hopscotch" third prize in Brady Senryu Contest (06); "old cat" first prize in Kaji Aso Haiku Contest (07); "arguing" third prize in HSA Brady Senryu Contest (06); "killing frost" Elizabeth Searle Lamb award in Kaji Aso Haiku Contest (08); "blizzard day" honorable mention in The Robert Speiss Memorial Haiku Contest (07); all others by permission of the author.

Raffael de Gruttola: "paw prints / disappear in the snow / wind under the hemlocks" Top Prize of Div. 1 First Yamadera Basho Memorial Museum English Haiku Contest. (09); "blues" from Mayfly winter (09); "contact lens" from Voice of the Cicada, Aug. (14); "hot walkers" from Voice of the Cicada; "drip, drip, drip," Voice of the Cicada; (14); "walking alone" from Wisteria Journal p 10; "at sundown" from Haiku Canada Anthology (14); "driftwood in sand" from Haiga portfolio: Echoes in Sand (09); "high on an American elm," from Voice of the Cicada; "caged hamster" from Voice of the Cicada; "mime " from Voice of the Cicada; "lost in the lights " Washington Post Editorial, Spring (08); "evening rush hour " from Ambrosia (08); "winter wake" from Voice of the Cicada; "floating up river" from Voice of the Cicada; "the great horned owl" from Voice of the Cicada; "deadened echoes" from Voice of the Cicada.

Gwenn Gurnack: "rain from the west" from Heron's Nest XIV:1 (12); "pock" from Heron's Nest XIV:2 (11); "lake trout rising" honorable mention in Kaji Aso Haiku Contest (11); "window flung wide" from Christian Science Journal (1/11); "Dad flicks a fly" from Acorn, Spring (13); "red oak leaf" from Heron's Nest XIV:3 (12); "boink" from Heron's Nest XV:2 (3); "empty fairground" from Heron's Nest XIII:3 (11); "in pre-dawn light" from Acorn Autumn (12); "evening star" from Frogpond 36:2 (13); "head over heels" honorable mention in in Kaji Aso Studio Haiku Contest (11); "vaulted stone cathedral" honorable mention in Rossinki Russian Anthology/Moscow Haiku Contest [tr. Z. Vayman] (12); "snowflakes" from Heron's Nest XV:4 (13); "rings" from Acorn Autumn (13); "still watching me" Museum of Haiku Literature Award, Frogpond 37:2 HSA(14); "her texted outrage" honorable mention in Kaji Aso Senryu Contest (12); all others by permission of the author.

Glenn Gustafson: "drops of rain" from *the ant's afternoon (90)*

Keith Heiberg: "the pallbearers" First Prize Kaji Aso Studio Haiku Contest, 2008.

Kay Higuchi: "the sun" from Modern Haiku 44.1.(13). All others by permission of the author.

Sarah Jensen: "knife through the apple" from *hands full of stars* (95)

Donald Kelly: "brilliant sun" from BHS chapbook *the ant's afternoon (90);*

Balasz Kosaras: "Fog over the lake" from *the ant's afternoon* (90)

Karen Klein: "retiree's garden" from Modern Haiku 39:3 (08); "vacant patio chairs" from South by Southeast 15:3 (08); "afternoon sky" from bottlerockets 19 (08). All others by permission of the author.

Jeannie Martin: "no path…" from *The Art of Awareness* (09); "reading alone" from *Clear Water: a haiku invitation into our luminous, sacred world* (13); "mountain hike" from *Clear Water: a haiku invitation into our luminous, sacred world;* "just when things seemed solid" from The Nor'Easter . All others by permission of the author.

Lauren Mayhew: "shooting star" from HRN XIII: 4 (11); "long stretch" from BR 14:1 (12); "hotel room" from BR 13:1 (11); "beach cottage" from Heron's Nest, XIII:4 (11); "garage sale" from Frogpond 36:2 (13); *"swing and a miss"* from Heron's Nest XIV:3 (12); "wet fallen leaves" from Nor'Easter, 17:2 (12); "forgiveness" from bottlerockets, 13:1 (11); "September dusk" from bottlerockets 28 (12); "first cold day" from Heron's Nest XIV:2 (12); "purple hues" from Modern Haiku 44:1 (13); "starless night" from bottlerockets 14:1 (12); "deep winter" from Nor'easter, 17:1 (12); "new year:" from Nor'easter, 17:2 (12); "city bus" from Frogpond 35:3 (12); "first warm day" from Heron's Nest, XIV:3 (12); "spring breeze," runner up in Haiku Calendar competition (13); "blue heron" from Nor'easter 17:1 and HAS Anthology (11). All others by permission of author.

Paul Mena: "old friends," "living," and "they say he has my eyes" from *moongarlic* 1:1 (13). All others by permission of author.

June Moreau: "wind shaping itself on the pond" and "my child's tears" from BHS chapbook *the ant's afternoon* (90). All others by permission of author.

Brett Peruzzi: "egret fishing" from F X:4 (87); "Autumn wind" from AC 3 (99); "Identifying" MH XX:2 (89); "behind the police station" from HN I:41 (12); "carnival midway" AC 3 (99); "A car's dragging muffler" from F XIII:87; "A phoebe's cry" from MH XXIII:3 (92). All others by permission of the author.

Bruce Ross: **"Sunlit clouds"** First Prize, Kaji Aso Studio Haiku Contest, 2006.

Larry Rungren All haiku by permission of the author.

David Shuster: "The doctor shakes her head" from *the ant's afternoon* (90).

Steven Small: "the barefoot girl" from *the ant's afternoon* (90)

Brenda Soyer: "will you still be here" from *windflow* (08)

Walter Valeri: "dusty window" and "sea-gull" from *windflow* (08)

Rich Youmans: "from the coiled" from *voice of the peeper (99)*.

John Ziemba : "the heft of an apple" from BHS chapbook *hands full of stars (95);* "below zero" from BHS chapbook *voice of the peeper (99);* inside the breaker *voice of the peeper (99);* all others by permission of author.

Made in the USA
Charleston, SC
14 December 2014